METATRON'S CODE

Demystifying Belief Systems

MARIE MARTIN, B.Msc.

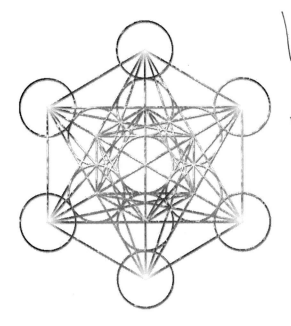

ALESIA PUBLISHING

Cover Art and Cover Designer: Soulscapes www.soulscapes.in
Back Cover Photographer: Ashly Narula
Inside Pages Illustrator: Ryan Ferguson

Publisher & Editor: Pamela Lynch, Alesia Publishing

ISBN: 978-1-9990394-0-0

DEDICATION

I dedicate this book to my children, Jason and Sam. They are my biggest teachers and loves.

I see my greatest achievement and inspiration every day in my children. They have taught me much, and I wouldn't be where I am today without them.

Special recognition goes to my Mum, Molly Tilson, my Sister, Jeanette Bedford, and Billy Martin. They are my biggest cheerleaders always!

THIS work is dedicated to each and every cell in the world around us that we can see, sense and so much more.

TABLE OF CONTENTS

PRAISE FOR METATRON'S CODE

"When I met Marie and she shared with me her healing vision for the world, I felt instant resonance and excitement! Everything she said felt like I was remembering an ancient truth about the world and I couldn't wait to learn more about what she had discovered. I was overjoyed when she shared this book with me! This is an important body of work that will help our species evolve to the next level of conscious awareness, by releasing the ancestral patterns of our past. I have never come across a system of healing quite as precise as Marie's. You won't be able to put this book down once you start!"

— *Joy Kingsborough*

"Marie! I'm brimming with happiness. Your words are delivered in such an easy and beautiful way, which spoke directly to my soul. I feel honoured and privileged that you shared your book with me and I will look forward to holding it in my hands. Seriously, I really love it, it's as if you've captured many of the important learnings that I've learnt and put them all together in a book!"

— *Kim Perry*

"This book gives some insight about the nature of beliefs. Through personal experiences, Marie explains how our beliefs directly impact our thoughts, observations, assumptions, and feelings to form a narrative which support the way we see ourselves and the world around us. In this book, Marie calls upon the reader to step through the practical exercise and untangle the current beliefs that are holding you from being your best version."

— *Shoeleh Forghani*

"The Metatron's Code will open your eyes to a new awareness of Belief Systems and much more. This is an inspiring collection of the author's personal stories and many scientific facts as well as various examples, tools and guides on how you can help yourself. Through her own experiences and those of her clients, Marie showcases how we can liberate ourselves and reclaim our true self-identity. If you are contemplating change within your life, this book will empower your journey with captivating information, knowledge and transformation."

— *Dagmara Staszak*

ACKNOWLEDGEMENTS

I acknowledge and show my appreciation for every individual cell. It is the intelligence within each cell of every living and innate being. I recognise and feel gratitude for every cell in existence. We are all connected in so many ways.

Thank you to all my family, friends, co-creators and mentors who have supported my journey. I like to be inclusive and, therefore, will not mention any by names. There are so many who have supported me in all dimensions, and it is impossible to recognise everyone. Those who have helped me the most know who they are and that I am truly grateful for them.

Thank you to the Universe for "downloading" this material to me over six years. It was a journey I will never forget and am deeply appreciative of!

PREFACE

Imagine the long-held beliefs that no longer serve you were debunked, dismantled, and dissolved. What would it mean for you to have freedom from thoughts that imprisoned you? Emotions that kept you turning away from the things you have been yearning for?

Imagine having the freedom to be you and to have the space for others.

Chapters three to eight explain the **six cognitive bodies**:

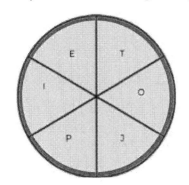

T - Thought/Intentions
O - Observation
J - Judgement
P - Perception
I - Internal Representation
E - External Representation

The chapters that follow demonstrate tools to re-write the redundant programming that binds you.

The balance of the book expands your **self-awareness**. The exercises help you **deepen your relationship with yourself** to create freedom in relationships with others.

INTRODUCTION

Brilliant! Finally, a way to demystify and re-create a belief.

The knowledge contained on these pages will help you decipher your belief system. You'll learn to deactivate the harmful ones and illuminate new beliefs.

Marie Martin first received information about the Metatron through her son's dreams. The downloads started once Marie realised he was not talking about Transformers. Well, he was, but not the same ones that came alive in the movie, "The Transformers."

Marie has identified the six bodies your belief is expressed through. They are in your Mental, Physical, Emotional, Spiritual, Internal and External bodies.

You cannot think your way through debunking your belief. You cannot feel, meditate, pray or chant a mantra and cause a belief to manifest into a new one. This book offers a simple solution to add to your practices to make it easier!

Marie guides you through each body to give you an awareness in your own beliefs. She helps you crack the code as you move through a process to transform your belief system.

Throughout the book, Marie illustrates how her understanding unfolded. There is an intricacy in our body's intelligence, and each belief is interwoven through the six bodies of the Metatron's Code.

She learned to be open and curious. She practised deep listening to hear the messages her body was receiving. This is both Marie's invitation and promise to you. With self-responsibility, you can become the energy master of your body. When you do, miracles happen.

Many of us have been together in other dimensions, and have tried to bring in these Sacred Texts. Now the world is more readily open to receive this information.

Marie has the distinct honour of being the first published author in the Alesia Library. Sacred Knowledge flowed through her for all of our benefits. It will help us re-remember and upgrade our beliefs to live inspired and limitless lives.

Let your journey to understanding the Metatron's Code continue. You are here to both witness and embrace your role in this Shift to Love.

Pamela Lynch
Alesia Publishing

Chapter 1

BELIEF IS MAGIC

It is true: BELIEF IS MAGIC!

This book is about to demystify Belief Systems and bring awareness to the importance of creating healthy beliefs.

Our beliefs can be very deeply rooted in our subconscious minds. We are often totally unaware of our beliefs and how they affect our lives. When we bring focus to our beliefs, we can bring them to awareness and begin to understand the world that we are creating around us.

If we can imagine it, we can visualise it. If we can visualise it, we can believe it. If we can believe it, we can create it. In fact, not only CAN we create it, when we BELIEVE, we absolutely DO create it!

Belief is the energy that manifests the person, place, thing and thought that we believe in.

We manifest, expand and become with BELIEF!

The belief is the SPARK, the way of life, how things happen, and how we create our core cellular information!

There are three different types of beliefs:

1. Belief in ALL that IS: God, Buddha, Mohammad, a Higher Power, or Universal Power of some type.

2. Belief in Self or Others.

3. Belief in creations of Thoughts and Intentions; Observations; Judgements; Perceptions; Internal Representations — how we see ourselves; External Representations — how we present ourselves to the world.

People who have established a strong belief in others, a higher power (God, Buddha, Mohammad) and/or themselves from an early age have much stronger foundations to support them through life.

When we have a belief in something, then we set the Thoughts/Intentions, Observations, Judgements, Perceptions, Internal Representations and External Representations into the cellular intelligence.

We refer to these as the six bodies. Keep in mind that all of these bodies must work together to produce results.

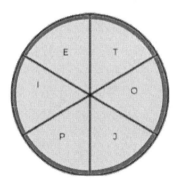

Cells Information
T - Thought/Intentions
O - Observation
J - Judgement
P - Perception
I - Internal Representation
E - External Representation

"There can be miracles, when we believe..."
- Whitney Houston -

NOT IF ... when. WHEN we believe, we can create anything — even miracles!

Churches have always known this, which is why they put significant importance on belief. My coach and mentor, Joy Kingsborough, told me the church changed the true meaning of Belief in the 13th Century.

*Before this date BELIEF meant to "***Love and Adore.***"*

The church changed it to "True and Proven." "You will believe in the church as it is a "True and Proven" doctrine.

With the original understanding of the word belief, the belief itself does not need to be true and proven. We love and adore the belief! Unfortunately, the 13th Century church lost the true definition of the word Belief and manipulated the meaning for its own purpose.

It didn't matter though. The vibration of the word cannot change! When you say "I believe" and make a decision to believe something, then the creation of that thing takes place.

The VIBRATION of a word cannot change!

When we have a collective belief in the same thing, it amplifies! Just as harmonic frequencies amplify and are greater when the two original sounds are combined.

We look for others to agree with us to amplify this process. If you and I believe the same thing, then we duplicate and amplify the belief. It brings it into existence even quicker!

A group of friends and I get together regularly for meditation evenings. We created a ritual around belief. Each person states their aspiration and belief, and then we all hold the belief for that person.

We collectively amplify that belief.

When we love the BELIEF, we observe the BELIEF, and the BELIEF creates. Remember when we have a collective belief, it amplifies!

Every belief we hold manifests in our life.

My sister, Jeanette, believes she can manifest anything, and she does. I call her a Master Manifestor because she can manifest anything seemingly out of thin air!

She says, "You just have to believe it is true and it happens!" She has a strong belief in the process and manifests the most amazing experiences.

It is crucial to increase awareness about the power we hold!

We all inherit both healthy and unhealthy belief systems from our ancestors. Our unhealthy Belief Systems are not real — they can be a whole heap of BS. Since we inherited them from our family, teachers or peers, they remind us of our loved ones. We want to keep our beliefs because they make us feel comfortable. Because of this entanglement, we "Love and Adore" them, so they form creation!

Remember, ALL beliefs started as helpful beliefs, even the seemingly unhelpful ones. You may ask, "Why would we create a belief around unworthiness?" Every belief created is for our protection to keep us safe.

Over time, our situations change. The beliefs we once had out of protection, we no longer need to protect us. We have a choice to upgrade the software around that old belief as it may be redundant. It is important for us to acknowledge that every belief at one time was perfect in its creation. We can create new helpful beliefs at any time!

A whole load of unhelpful BS can trap and trip us, and the people around us, in self-sabotaging ways! Why is that?

Why do we self-sabotage in life?

We know our Belief Systems are coded directly into our subconscious mind in Theta state (roughly between the ages of 0-7). A large percentage of that programming is self-sabotaging. Our programming starts with our Mother's thoughts and belief systems in vitro! I often heard my Aunty Joan say, "It's very important to be happy and calm in pregnancy.

A happy and calm Mother makes a happy and calm baby!" It turns out she is right!

I studied **Conversational Intelligence®** with the late Neuroscientist, Judith E. Glasier. Her work scientifically proves that the chemicals created from being in a happy state stimulate growth hormones and telomeres. These are the compound structures at the end of a chromosome linked to ageing. A happy state activates the prefrontal cortex which floods the brain, and therefore the body, with oxytocin, serotonin, and dopamine! The happy, peaceful, growth chemicals! [1]

We understand now that although we are in a physical reality, we know that 99.999% of everything is actually space! So what is in that space? Dr Bruce Lipton states there are only three things that can change a cell's structure: **Toxins, Trauma or Thought**! What if the ingredient in that 99.999% space is thought or intention?

[1] *Used by permission from* **Conversational Intelligence®** *and the work of Judith E. Glaser.*

Chapter 2

CREATION OF CELLS

I had a client a few years ago, who we will call Susan. I dropped her into a hypnotic state and she travelled very far to a place seemingly before time. As a child Susan could "zoom in", and we explored this ability. She travelled right into the cells and repeated, "triangle, circle, square" while she heard a chime and saw a flash of light.

I believe she was communicating with the cells and seeing how they were "coded" or created. She saw these shapes, saw a spark of light, then heard a chime, and the structure of the cells would change state. In this hypnotic journey, she received communication that the cells were sad and were not acknowledged.

Our cells communicate with each other through their own language of chemical signals. I dreamt about how the cells communicate with each other. I was shown a Connect Four game as a simple way of demonstrating conduction. In this game drop red or yellow discs to form four colours in a row to win the game. I was shown that you drop energy into a cell and that transfers to the next cell and the next cell, etc. Imagine the sadness bouncing from cell to cell! Now imagine appreciative energy being dropped into a cell and watch that bounce from cell to cell to cell for all eternity.

When we acknowledge and appreciate each and every cell, we are able to be in a healthier and happier state!

This symbol of the triangle, circle, and square has repre-sented alchemy and the Philosopher's Stone since the 17th Century. It means "attempting anything seems possible." The Philosopher's Stone is a legendary alchemic substance that can turn base metals into gold or silver. It is also called the Elixir of Life, useful for rejuvenation and for achieving immortality! The Philosopher's Stone symbolises perfection, enlightenment, and heavenly bliss.

Discovering the Philosopher's Stone was known as The Great Work or, in Latin, Magnum Opus!

Is it possible that what Susan was seeing in this journey was the creation of cells taking form? I discussed this with a friend, Ryan Ferguson, and he had an amazing take on this information. Here are his thoughts around this communication:

"On any geometric grid, imagine that each point is self-aware, but lines connect them. When a single point of consciousness expands to a second point, we only have a line but no shape. As soon as there is a third point, we get a triangle. If that triangle recognises its duality, then it sees its mirror image, and it doubles to form a square. If that square then doubles on a third axis and rotates, the points will form a sphere. This consciousness continues to expand into more and more points of consciousness to take us into greater and greater complexity of sacred geometry. The fractal nature of consciousness. I believe that the creator is sad because too many have lived in self-imposed isolation from it. No need to worry though, the algorithms to achieve balance have already been written." Ryan expanded on the information that Susan and I received in that session.

I received my own information about cellular space. Each cell has its own intelligence in the form of a BELIEF. This belief is created in the form of Thoughts and Intentions,

Observations, Judgements, Perceptions, Internal Representations, and External Representations. Remember, Internal Representation is how you see yourself, and External Representation is how you present yourself to the world.

Notice the shape at the bottom of each page.

It is known as a **Metatron's Cube** in Sacred Geometry.

Metatron historically is recognised as an Archangel, who is known as the **Angel of Life**. He achieved a level of enlightenment or understanding. This led to his physical body transitioning into a higher dimension. The pursuit of alchemy promised to transmute matter into a higher energy state. Many spiritual leaders are documented as having a similar transition.

In the following six chapters, we will explore each of these bodies in the intentional order I was introduced to them.

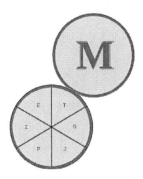

Chapter 3

THE MENTAL BODY

Beliefs are stored in the Mental Body within Neuro Pathways.

I studied Neuro-Linguistic Programming with Steve Boyley from NLP Mind, and learned how these thoughts sit in the Neuro Pathways! I took a Practitioner's course in NLP and spent a year practising these tools on myself. After that, I returned to study the Master Practitioner Course and spent another year focusing on my beliefs. I paid attention to the energy around my thoughts and filtered and reframed my toxic thoughts in my belief systems. I then assisted others to reframe their belief systems.

Our thoughts are just that, thoughts.

They are not real, but they do have energy. They are not real, but they can create. They are not real, but if we believe them to be real, they can cause harm. They are not real, but if we believe it, they can heal.

How are you choosing your thoughts? Are they helpful or unhelpful? Take care of your thoughts and what they are creating for yourself and the outside world.

We see our world externally filtered by the lens of our own focus — it's like wearing glasses of a different shade. If we think blue thoughts, we see the world through these blue lenses. If we think rose coloured then, yes, we see a rose-coloured world!

We must have an awareness of what our filters are in order to change them. That, of course, is the challenge as they sit in our subconscious mind! The good news is that we are receiving communication from the outside world all the time. We are receiving communication that is showing us what our beliefs are. We have to listen up and pay attention.

When we pay attention, we become self-aware!

There are clues to this higher awareness in our history. When the Egyptians mummified bodies, they carefully wrapped the heart placing it back in the body and threw away the brains.

HeartMath® is an organisation that has been studying heart intelligence for years now. They have proven that the heart actually receives information before the brain does! In a double-blind experiment, people were exposed to images with either calming or disturbing impressions. The heart responded appropriately to the impression BEFORE the images were shown. How is that possible? It seems that our hearts can predict what is about to be experienced.

There are six brains as demonstrated by the late Judith E. Glasier. Her brilliant Neuroscience work with **Conversational Intelligence®** shows which chemicals are produced, where they are produced in the brains, and the cause and effect of those chemicals. [2]

The six brains are connected.

Imagine the possibility if the information begins with our heart, and living in our heart gives us the latest updates.

[2] *Used by permission from* **Conversational Intelligence®** *and the work of* **Judith E. Glaser.**

The **Heart-Brain** enables us to connect all of our internal systems and allows us to connect with others.

The **Primitive Brain** is hardwired to protect us and how we react to threats.

The **Limbic Brain** stores a history of all emotional experiences.

The **Neocortex** is hardwired for language. It stores information and basic reasoning (cognitive skills that enable us to navigate our day).

The **Prefrontal Cortex** is hardwired for higher-level coordination of the whole brain. [3]

The Microbiota-**Gut-Brain** is a fast growing field of research, with fascinating findings.

It has been discovered that 90% of serotonin is produced by the gut bacteria. Happy gut. Happy person!

[3] *Used by permission from* **Conversational Intelligence®** *and the work of* **Judith E. Glaser.**

Chapter 4

THE PHYSICAL BODY

The connection to my own physical body was a slow discovery!

Adrenal Fatigue and Hypothyroidism made life difficult for me, and I knew I had to start moving. I could barely lift my head off the sofa after 5 PM each night and literally had to drag my body out of bed each morning. It was exhausting! Any exercise I attempted caused flu-like symptoms the next day, which is a common symptom of Adrenal Fatigue.

Even though I consistently felt sick, I started walking. A friend taught me running techniques, which was quite challenging since I lived on a mountain. Soon I started interval running, and put those new techniques into practice. Before long I could run 5 km at high elevation even with the thin, clean mountain air!

Then I was 'asked' to do more.

I woke up at 5 AM every morning and set off up the mountain with my dog!

The mountain is fairly remote, and I would rarely see anyone on my daily morning journey. I practised changing my mental thoughts on the way up, shifting the old toxic ones. I needed this alone time to reflect, to understand my way of thinking and beliefs.

I would stop at a tree three-quarters of the way up. It wasn't a particularly pretty tree, given its damaged top but it was MY tree! I would sit and meditate by this tree. I'd talk to it, tell it stories, and have a rest before I set off on my journey.

My son asked me if I wanted to join the Chairlift Challenge at the ski resort where we lived. It's a race to the top of every chairlift on the mountain. Since I was running the trail anyway, I said, "Yes, let's do it!"

I set a goal to get my time under two hours even though

I had never thought of myself as a runner. The fact that I even considered entering the challenge was a miracle in itself! The year before I was on the obesity scale and not coping physically well at all.

We set off that Autumn morning. The challenge was on a trail in the opposite direction of my usual run, so "my tree" was on the downside of the trail. My son and I were running well and enjoying this journey together, when all of a sudden I thought, "Where is my tree?" I looked up and saw it was right in front of me! As I looked up, I lost my footing on the rough mountain terrain. I went over on my ankle, sprained it badly and couldn't stand on it at all.

As I sat at my tree in tears, nursing my pain, I realised it wasn't a coincidence that this incident happened right at this particular tree on a day when I had access to emergency services. Remember, most days I wouldn't see a single person on the mountain while I was running!

I sat for a while wondering, and got curious. "What was the lesson here for me?"

I sent my son down the mountain, assuring him that if I needed help, I would call him. Then I dropped into the space in my ankle and had a conversation with it right there on the trail at my tree! I made a deal with my pain. I knew there was a message for me in this injury. I acknowledged my ankle for showing up for me in this way and creating a situation for me to understand. I was compassionate with my injury and gave it attention.

"I know you have a message for me, and that this incident is a gift. I know that there is gold in this gift, but right now you have to give me some time to finish this race."

In my mind, I put this gift in a box, beautifully wrapped it, and finished it off with a big red bow. I put it on an imaginary shelf to open it later and receive the gift inside! Satisfied that I would go back to receive the information, my ankle relaxed a little.

I stood and put my weight on my ankle slowly and found it could hold my weight. I thanked it profusely. I thanked "my tree" also for the gift.

My walk turned into a run, taking care to watch my step, I finished that challenge in ONE HOUR and FORTY-FIVE MINUTES. My time was only FIVE MINUTES behind my son who was waiting for me and cheered me through the finish line! I was a cool Mum that day!

When I got home, I remembered to take the gift off the imaginary shelf and unwrapped the package to receive the gift of information inside. Yes, my ankle was sore for a few days, but it healed a lot quicker than expected!

While cooking dinner the next week, I burnt my arm on the element of our oven. "Ouch!"

Hmmm … time to put my new knowledge into practice! I ran my arm under cold water and then went to a quiet room where I put all my attention on the burn. I set the intention to receive the information in the gift my body had to tell me.

I dropped my awareness into the burn. It seared with pain! I stayed with it though, not resisting, not trying to ignore it, or make it go away. I felt into the burn, gave it attention, and had a conversation with it.

I did this for as long as I could stand the pain.

I'd take a break. Drop right back into it and stay with it again.

Be with it. Be friends with it.

I did this over and over again until I "received" the core message.

When I went to bed that night, the pain had disbursed. Miraculously, when I awoke the next morning, there was only the tiniest mark on my arm. I couldn't believe it!

Being with the burn, sitting with it, paying attention, receiving the information, and communicating with it had actually HEALED THE BURN almost completely!

These experiences made me realise that the physical body, as well as the mental body, requires attention.

Louise Hay's book, *Heal Your Life*, lists the Metaphysical cause for a physical ailment and an affirmation to overcome it.

The first time I read that book, I looked at all the ailments other people had and noted the belief around the ailment was pretty much spot on with that person. Then, with my commitment to my own journey of self-awareness, I reread it. This time with my own ailments in mind, I had to admit the metaphysical beliefs attached to those ailments were also true for me.

Adrenal Fatigue:
Defeatism. No longer caring for self. Anxiety.

Hypothyroidism:
Giving up, feeling hopelessly stifled.

After the initial sting of the realisation that these beliefs were probably true for me, I set to work on all the beliefs I could come up with around these words. They were plentiful!

Believing you can heal is the key.

My Step-Dad told me a story about a man he knew who was diagnosed with terminal cancer and given weeks to live. Not surprisingly, his weight and health dropped dramatically that week and was literally dying in front of his family's eyes. A week later he was told that he had been misdiagnosed and he was actually one hundred percent clear! The man recovered overnight and went back to being the happy, vibrant, energetic man that he had been before his diagnosis!

When he believed he was dying, he was. When he believed he was well, he WAS!

I know this is an extreme case, but there are lots of examples of this where people have had a Near Death Experience and come back to life with the belief that they have been healed, and miraculously they are! Doctors call this

Spontaneous Remission.

We are the Kings and Queens of our king-doms.

The kingdoms are made up of billions of cells that are here for one purpose and one purpose alone — to keep us alive and well! We are the masters of our kingdoms, yet we mostly ignore the cells that keep us alive. We don't communicate enough with our bodies.

When was the last time you woke up and said "Good Morning" to yourself? Imagine if you ignored your partner in the same way. What reaction would you get from them?

Imagine how alone our cells are feeling in our bodies! Abandoned by their leader.

Dr Emoto's work shows the difference in water cells frozen with different intentions.

Cells with loving intentions create the most beautiful images. The ones with harmful intentions create images where the cells look harmed! Our bodies consist of over 70% water!

Imagine what we are creating in our own bodies by not having loving thoughts.

Get this: The cells that are ignored deteriorate the quickest!

Did you know that some molecules don't even get activated until they are observed?

Imagine what is inside you that you haven't yet activated. The possibilities are endless, and far beyond our limited human capacity to comprehend at this point.

This evidence clearly demonstrates that ignoring the cells in our bodies literally causes them to deteriorate. Ignoring the cells in our bodies is like neglecting a whole kingdom of beings and then expecting them to work diligently for you and keep your body healthy.

Then we get sick and wonder why? Of course, nutrition also plays a huge role in how healthy our body and mind is. Although serotonin is well known as a brain neurotransmitter, it is estimated that 90 percent of the body's serotonin is made in the digestive tract. Therefore if our gut bacteria is happy, then we have a ninety percent greater chance of being happy!

I encourage you to educate yourself on an exercise and nutrition regimen that works for you.

Chapter 5

THE EMOTIONAL BODY

The Emotional Body allows us to feel our emotions. Like all other bodies, it also requires attention.

Dr David Hawkins created a map of the emotional scale called the **Map of Consciousness©**. It illustrates that any emotion under the "frequency" of 200 is below the Line of Integrity. These emotions are out of integrity, and thus not accurate!

You have heard the acronym for FEAR — False Evidence Appearing Real!

We can FEEL into the belief with the help of our Emotional Body.

Unhelpful beliefs are under the line of integrity. They are just not true, but they feel true, so we believe that they are accurate!

Our unhelpful beliefs have lower frequencies. They are under the line of integrity. It is not for us to have judgements of those lower level emotions, or the people experiencing them.

Every level has its purpose, and we are all in different stages of our journey. We can hold the belief that anyone has all the resources they need to elevate from one level to another. We can help people by keeping that belief for them. Having someone else believe in you amplifies the possibility of leaping from one level to another!

It is good practice to become friends with the Emotional Body. Often we judge the lower level emotions as bad. Emotions are emotions, neither good or bad.

Practice feeling into the frequency that you are experiencing.

Sometimes the first emotion that we feel is not the core

emotion. It is good to ask what this belief feels like, then keep asking, "What is the LEVEL of this emotion you are feeling. What is the emotional level underneath this?"

Ask until you know you can't go any further, and you run out of levels. Either that or you begin to notice the neutral feelings or higher level emotions. We can have a conversation with the core emotion. Ask if there is a message to receive. We can acknowledge the message and thank it for showing us our beliefs through our feelings.

Our feelings are our internal map, directing us to show us how we feel about our beliefs. They show us how we feel about ourselves internally. They show us what feelings we are projecting externally to the world!

Notice when you are feeling a lower vibrational feeling that you have lower vibrational thoughts.

NO EXCEPTION!

We can drop into the lowest level of emotion. Feel it. Play with it. Acknowledge it. Thank it for its wisdom.

Appreciate it for showing you gently, what you feel about your beliefs. Now you have space to choose a new feeling. It is empowering to understand you have a choice.

We are often taught as children that it is wrong to express our emotions. We are asked to stop crying even when we feel the need to do so.

When my kids were toddlers, I'd reassure them that it was ok to cry. I remember my friend was surprised because it was the first time she'd heard a Mum encouraging their children to cry.

It feels alien to explore our feelings at first. Ignoring them feels worse. I'm asking you to investigate your emotions now. Dive in deep and swim in the wonderful world that is waiting for you there!

Chapter 6

THE SPIRITUAL BODY

The Spiritual Body is how we gain an under-standing of stories supporting our beliefs.

Once we have understanding, we have awareness. We can see the pattern of "stories" created over time. When we start seeing patterns, we usually see them in others first. "Why does that person keep attracting the same type of partner?"

"Why does that person keep having the same pattern around money?"

When we notice the patterns in others, then we can't help but begin to wonder if those patterns also occur in our life.

You may have thoughts such as, *"Hmmm...is the same thing happening to me? Is this why I attract the same type of situations with a partner, friend, or money?"*

I worked with a client who wanted to spend the hour session telling me, in great depth, about his story. I had an understanding of the belief creating HIS story (*HIStory*). I asked if we could work on the belief before he finished his story. He reluctantly accepted as he was quite in the swing of this dramatic event.

We worked on the belief, and I was now quite prepared to listen to the rest of his story.

"No," he said, *"I don't need to, the story isn't relevant anymore."*

Just like that, his story had lost all its force!

What stories are you telling at great length to whoever will listen? Watch your stories. They are giving you a sign of what your beliefs are.

Watch how you "play life."

Observe how you play during competition. How you be-have in sports or games is usually the same way you will act in life, relationships, and business!

Do you play fair during competition? If you do, you will gen-erally play fair in life.

Beliefs are sometimes created in another dimensional space and *"brought forward."* At times we need to drop into the Entry Point of the dimensional space. We then dis-solve the story at the very beginning of its creation.

Sometimes it is enough to become aware that the story and patterns exist for it to shift your belief. That light bulb moment or AHA moment is enough to shift the thought to something new. The realisation to shift into a different awareness altogether.

Sometimes the beliefs are not our own.

They are "inherited" from previous generations, and are car-ried forward to future generations if we do not deal with them now. Beliefs continue through seven generations!

Mirror Neurons: we mirror what we see.

In my studies of Neuro-Linguistic Programming, I learned

about Mirror Neurons. As babies, we learn through our mirror neurons.

Thus we mirror belief systems also! We mirror the emotions, thoughts and belief systems that our parents have. We take on emotions and thoughts (beliefs) that are not ours. They are our parents' beliefs.

I remember my Dad having a certain look sometimes when I wasn't in his favour. Dad passed away a few years ago. I was walking through a park when I *saw* him right in front of me with this particular look on his face. When he had that look, I thought he disliked me, but at that moment I saw the truth and burst into tears on the spot. It wasn't that he disliked me at all. He disliked himself!

My mirror neurons reflected the emotion. I mirrored the emotion and felt it. I misinterpreted the emotion being directed towards me, and took it personally and believed it! I thought my Dad didn't like me my whole life! Once I had finished mopping up the tears, I raced home to tell my children.

I said over and over, "*IF you ever see an expression on my face that is not loving, please, please do NOT take it personally! It is NOT directed at you; it is how I AM FEELING internally!*"

They looked at me as if I had horns growing out of my head.

"What on earth are you talking about Mum? You never look like you dislike me."

Perhaps my approach was unnecessary, but I had to make sure that they understood the message.

We must see the truth in how others are presenting themselves.

If we take it personally and believe that it is directed at us, we can start a war on the spot!

If I had understood it was my Dad's insecurities that were showing, then I could have saved us both a world of pain. I could have realised that my Dad needed more love and understanding. I could have saved myself the shame of believing that my Dad disliked me!

Our mirror neurons are brilliant, but we need to be aware of how destructive our thoughts can be! They can turn a loving relationship into a war zone in a split decision. And for my Dad and I, it did. We had a war against each other for years. This could have ended in seconds (and did) with a little more awareness and understanding!

It's not only emotions that we take on board from our peers, but we also pick up their state of health and well-being. I want to introduce Dr Bruce Lipton's work on Epigenetics.

Dr Lipton outlines the connection between our experiences and our genetic code. This process is called epigenetics, and it shook the world of genetics when uncovered. Before that, it was a held belief that our genetics never changed. We were stuck with the cards we were dealt. Thanks to Dr Lipton, we no longer believe that to be true.

When I was diagnosed with Hypothyroidism, the Doctor told me that I would be on medication for the rest of my life. I responded to him, "*That is an interesting belief! I choose not to have that same belief.*"

He laughed, and replied, "*Oh! You are one of those types of people, are you? Well, believe this: YOU WILL BE ON MEDICATION for the rest of your life.*"

At that moment, I chose to throw that belief straight in the bullshit bin and did. I do value doctors, by the way, and I continue to get my Thyroid levels tested. But I did not need to believe that I would be on medication for the rest of my life.

I always recommend going to see your doctor for conditions. Yet, I also believe a significant percentage of healing is within you! Look at all the blind test results with placebos. Drug trials show case studies where the people who took a sugar pill instead of the actual medication had the same health improvements! They believed they were taking the real medication!

I was at a party in my earlier days, and my friend wasn't feeling well. She wanted to go home and had a cold developing. It was late, and we were supposed to be staying overnight at the house party, and we couldn't get a taxi home. My friend wanted a pharmaceutical drink to feel better, and there was no medication at all in the house. I mixed a little sugar, flour and water and gave it to her. She drank the whole thing in one gulp, shuddered a little, and said, "that feels better." Shortly after that, she went to sleep for the night! It probably wasn't so nice of me to do that, but it worked, and we laugh about it now!

I found out all the beliefs around the illness of Hypothyroidism, and I began to work on them one at a time. Unravelling the internal mess that I had created so I could start to write a new inner story ... a much healthier one!

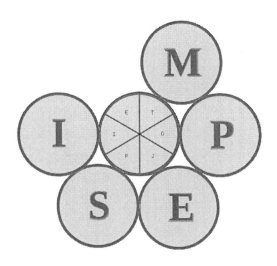

Chapter 7

THE INTERNAL BODY

Besides the raging war with others, we can also create a conflict within ourselves.

I took on the belief from my Dad that he didn't like me. Therefore, I formed an idea that I was "unlikeable," and "disliked!"

Consequently, thoughts of dislike created the internal war that broke down all my bodies one at a time. Self-sabotage and self-destructive beliefs made me my own worst enemy!

If I were to ever speak to my friends in the same way I had

been talking to myself, I would be quite surprised if they were still my friends.

I was insulting myself daily. My bruised, abused soul was leaving me and refusing to come back! It was finding any way it could to escape from this internal war!

The escapism started young, and my favourite was going into fantasy land. I could daydream for hours at a time. Often the fantasy was far more enjoyable than what was going on right in front of me. Acceptance was not my greatest skill; it took years to accept myself or my current situation!

As an empath, I "took on" other people's emotions. I would feel them. I then attempted to carry it for them, so that they wouldn't need to carry it. I thought I was strong enough to carry it all. What I didn't realise is that when I willingly took their "backpack" of loaded BS, I duplicated it. So now we were both carrying the backpacks, and the weight doubled, pulling us both down.

Be a responsible empath.

To be a responsible empath, we feel the feeling to understand it, but we must learn to release it. Once we do and let it flow through us, we can hold space without holding the weight of the world!

A couple of years ago I went shopping with my son. He noticed as we were loading the car that I was a little grumpy. He said, "Mum, you have eight coats on."

I looked at him and asked, "What do you mean? It is the middle of the summer."

He replied, "You went around the supermarket taking everyone's stuff, like a coat...I will take your stuff. I will take your stuff. And yours, too.

Now you have eight coats of other people's stuff. Take them off and send them to the recycling. They are not yours!"

I laughed out loud; he was right. I hadn't taken care of my energy while shopping, and I had picked up other people's energetic "stuff."

I intentionally cleared my energy field, taking off the coats and sending them to recycling. I felt much lighter for it!

Wish I had that much wisdom at such an early age!

I started biting my nails as a child. "Eating them away to the quick" as they would say in Northern England, where I was born and raised. This led to other tendencies: smoking, drinking, unhealthy relationships. I made the excuse that it was ok; everyone else was doing it! And isn't that indeed the shame of the story? Almost everyone WAS doing it, so I thought it was normal.

I thought it was normal to numb out the world with romance novels. Endless movies, drinking, eating, shopping, browsing social media for hours on end — *anything* to assist me in leaving my body just for a while. To blanket in the comfort and quiet to escape that incessant internal war. The war that is so deafeningly loud you can't hear it.

Have you noticed that call to attention from Netflix after three episodes? "Are you STILL watching?"

Who is judging who here?

Where has our society gone wrong?

I remember watching a movie in the '90s called *Trainspotting*, where a young Ewan McGregor said, "Choose Life."

"Choose mind-numbing, spirit-crushing game shows. Choose the BIG TV … OR CHOOSE LIFE!"

It was the morning that I woke up feeling so bad, so unhealthy, so "Mind-Numbingly Spirit Crushingly bad" that I had THE CRASH!

I had to make a decision, and I am glad to say that I chose to end the internal war of "dis-ease" and CHOOSE LIFE instead, and started living!

Remember what story we are playing internally is etched on our faces and visible in our body language. We think we are hiding our internal pain. In fact, it is clear to others exactly what we are thinking and feeling.

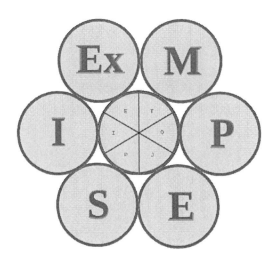

Chapter 8

THE EXTERNAL BODY

Our External Body is how we communicate to the world!

When I was running down the mountain, I was absorbing the communication from nature, and this communication was exuded out to the world.

This happens to all of us, which is why it's so important to spend time in nature.

Everything about us communicates to the world:

- Our body posture.
- Our facial expressions.
- The colour of our hair.
- The colour of our eyes and skin.
- Our body size and shape.
- How tall or small.
- What we wear and how we wear it.

Everything! Each cell communicates who we are and what our internal beliefs are.

Psychological research HAD classified six facial expressions. They correspond to distinct emotions: disgust, sadness, happiness, fear, anger, surprise. [4]

I find it interesting to see that four out of the six are perceived as negative emotions. A more recent researcher from Ohio State University found that humans actually have **21 different facial expressions**. A considerable jump from the six emotions noted before.

When we look in the mirror at ourselves, we are in observational mode.

[4] Reference: Black, Yacoob, 95

We don't see how we are when we're thinking specific thoughts. Have you ever watched a video of yourself not knowing you are being observed? It catches you off guard, and you think, "That doesn't look like me!"

I remember filming my kids and observing on the replay that my breathing was laboured. It struck me how fatigued I was, and I hadn't even realised it.

The way we feel is apparent in our facial expressions and physical appearance, even our breathing!

We know that up to 93% of communication is nonverbal! Body language, the tone of voice, body positioning all come into play. To focus only on the language we use is like watching only the conductor of a symphony.

Remember mirror neurons? When we are experiencing low vibrational thoughts, people can sense that. Our energy, facial features, and body language reflect that vibration.

We can sense others internal story. When someone walks into a room, you can feel whether they are happy or sad in an instant.

Our automatic programming comes into play.

Our brains begin searching for the meaning of that person's body language. What is the meaning of that facial expression or tone of voice? Our mind then informs us how to react to this situation. It searches for the "best-fit" file for this experience.

This "best-fit file" is based on the programming you had at the time of creation. Its match may be running on programming so old that it can't even be updated! Sometimes it has to be completely scrapped, and "new software" written! Imagine running an iPhone 8 on iPhone 4 software. It wouldn't work.

I had a conversation with a client once about the colour yellow. Her mother told her a story at a young age based on scientific research she had read. This study had shown that the colour yellow was the one most picked by people in a mental institution. She held the belief that if you wore this colour, it meant you were mentally ill! Believing this to be true, my client avoided wearing yellow ever, and people who wore that colour for obvious reasons!

That program had to be scrapped entirely. There are no amount of updates that can correct that programming into a healthy state. Together we "re-wrote" the program. She now believes that people wearing the colour yellow are "sunny" and feels safe approaching them! Luckily, once she was aware that she had this belief, she found it ludi-crously funny!

The alarming part of this story was that her programming was so deeply ingrained.

Without awareness, the belief was running on automatic.

We run on automatic programming roughly 90% of the time. We are almost entirely unaware of what our pro-grammed beliefs are! It is with self-awareness that you begin to realise these beliefs. Then you start to understand how untrue (and self-destructive) they actually can be!

Certain chemicals are produced in our brain and body when we feel unsafe. Every time she saw people wearing the colour yellow, or even saw the colour, she would be on high alert and feel unsafe. We changed the programming to "sunny". She now feels safe with the colour yellow and people wearing it. Thanks to our mirror neurons, those peo-ple would feel safe around her also.

Bizarre how we fence ourselves in to protect ourselves.

How are you fencing yourself in with your external projection to the world? Are you projecting beliefs that are safe or unsafe, kind or unkind, loving or unloving?

If we have unkind thoughts, we are projecting unkind thoughts! If you are harsh with yourself, you are harsh with others. If you are hard on yourself, you are projecting externally and being hard on others.

NO EXCEPTION!

We cannot be unkind to ourselves internally and be kind to others externally!

We can try, but it never quite hits the mark. It's never quite authentic enough, and it feels like a lie. We are not genuine enough. I have a program, *Finding You and Living True©*. We look at our beliefs and how to rewrite it to a healthy state. We can become authentic with ourselves and others.

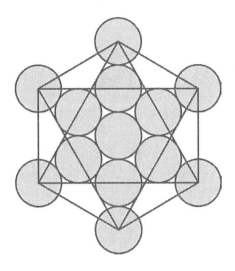

Chapter 9

THE ENTANGLEMENT

The cellular information becomes entangled in the six bodies.

Whether the belief is helpful or unhelpful, the same entanglement exists.

I see it like fine silver threads of spider's web that over time become dusty, heavy and even more entangled. Incidentally, woven into this thread is the hexagram, a six-pointed star. The hexagram represents the balance of masculine and feminine energies. It is the higher and lower aspects of self, two levels of reality representing all truth.

"As Above So Below!"

The Hexagram in Sacred Geometry is also the symbol of the heart chakra!

We ALL have the ability to "download" information.

I understand that when we change a belief, we also have to change it in all six bodies. Otherwise, the process is incomplete. I have a desire that all practitioners develop a practice of working in all six bodies.

This pattern sets, and we cast out a web to create the cellular belief into being. We call out for people, animals, nature, objects, environments, experiences, and places to support us in our core belief. Then the pattern is complete, and it becomes "true." We get our *supporting actors* to come into the movie that we have created for ourselves. The film plays out in our lives, and then it is confirmed as true. SO IT IS!

The belief is now 'true.' The movie is shown to us, and the patterns start to create. Have you ever been in a situation where you think you understand what is happening in the moment? Then you receive more information. This new information can completely change your perspective of that moment.

The belief is formed and sets into a dimensional form. It is no longer 3D or linear. It becomes a dimensional aspect that is created on a quantum level.

After that, the pattern reproduces more of the same over and over again. The automatic programs and patterns begin. They won't be interrupted again until we bring them to our full awareness for reassessment.

Most of us are too busy with life. Too busy with businesses, families and dramas. Too busy for self-awareness of the patterns created. The patterns build and recreate, one on the top of the other, on top of the other, on top of the other. We are amplifying the patterns. The patterns get bigger, louder, more uncomfortable, and more painful for us to endure.

The patterns are asking us to pay attention, slow down, look at the pain, but we are far too busy for that. We have far more important things to do! And it takes more and more to drown out the noise and numb us into maintaining the belief that everything is ok!

Of course, these patterns are just patterns. They are not intended to be painful.

It is only our human judgement of the creation that makes it *right or wrong, pleasant or painful, peaceful or warlike.*

The belief creates whatever YOU put in the middle of the cell. It is YOUR CHOICE. The whole pattern is set into motion.

The Universal Laws have no judgment.

What you put into the cells' information and set in this pattern creates, regardless!

It is only us who makes that creation perceivably good or bad. But it is neither good nor bad. IT JUST IS. Everything happens FOR us, not TO us.

We create input by choice, and that choice creates things for us.

We then have a choice to judge it as *good or bad*, to *ignore it*, *keep it*, or *change it*! But know this, although it is hard to believe, we always have a choice. NO EXCEPTION!

We pride ourselves on manifesting the things we want. If we don't like the experience, we think surely we didn't manifest THAT! Maybe we didn't choose that EXACT experience, BUT we did choose the belief that was triggered.

Remember these choices are subconscious.

If we have unworthy beliefs, then we have experiences that play out and trigger our lack of worthiness.

If this pattern creates over and over again, it becomes more complex and dense. It creates over and over and over and adds more energy to it each time. See the diagram below of the Metatron's Cube replicating over and over and over.

Metatron's Cube shares 2-D resonance with the Flower of Life, another well-known fractal of sacred geometry. It is the basis for the creation of all nature!

Or as I imagine, it looks something more like an atom!

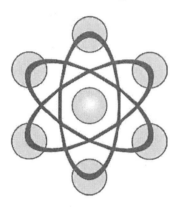

We create our reality based on the information we put into our cells ... it IS OUR CREATION.

We are the creators of our own life.

Of course, we have to be compassionate and forgiving with ourselves. Remember our 0-7 year-old mind programs most of these cells.

We may not be conceived with unconditional love, but the spark of life IS unconditional. The programming begins in Vitro. We are "programmed" by people who were programmed by THEIR 0-7 year-old mind. Who were programmed by people who were programmed by THEIR 0-7 year-old mind ... and so on and so on ... back through seven generations. It's our generation plus six others!

It is up to us what we do with this awareness. We can change generational beliefs. We can explore, identify and acknowledge them. We can decide whether we want to keep them or replace them. When we pick up the generational beliefs we also often take on the ailments that go with that belief. We can often heal genetic diseases by healing the beliefs that create ailments in the first place!

This is what I did with Hypothyroidism. Yes, it is a genetic condition that runs in my family. I chose to work on the beliefs surrounding this illness and healed the disease!

We all have the power to do this!

We can take self-responsibility to look at the information we have coded into the cell. We can choose whether we like it or not. Are we willing to change what we do not like? If we ARE willing, then we have a decision to make. We can change it and transform it into something we do like!

When we do work on our own beliefs, we can then unchain from the ancestral lineage. We can heal for all time, perceived past, present and future. We can heal for the past generations. We can prevent this belief from being cast forward into future generations.

Whatever we are looking at in the here and now we are

seeing from our past experience.

The *Course of Miracles* demonstrates this well. It's a collection of daily practices that shows us that our current reality is not at all real. It can be confronting to follow these practices, but it does expand your perception.

We humans are particularly good at distracting ourselves!

When you get too good at distracting yourself, find someone to help you.

Why would we distract ourselves? Well, sometimes we get comfortable with what is.

If a particular behaviour is all we have known, then we get comfortable with it. Even if that behaviour is seemingly unhelpful to us, it still feels comfortable.

We become uncomfortable about changing beliefs. This is because we do not know what life will be like without them. Change isn't always comfortable even if it is for our benefit! The process of growth and change can be uncomfortable. Crustaceans and arachnids demonstrate this well. First, they must discard the husk that they called home. Then push through the vulnerability of having no shell until the new one begins to form.

I have had clients who had beliefs chosen from their own experience and BOTH genetic lines! These beliefs are pretty well ingrained and require assistance to transmute!

The patterns are in the perfectly simple yet brilliantly complex form of the Metatron's Cube.

The pattern is asking us to reassess the cellular information. Reassess to see if the data is still applicable, if it can be upgraded, or re-written. It's like someone knocking on your door knowing you are inside. They will knock louder and louder and be more persistent until you are willing to open the door.

It is an invitation to look inside!

It is a much easier process to look at this information for clarity and understanding. Most of us continue to ignore the messages, signals and internal shouting asking us to pay attention.

Until THE CRASH HAPPENS....

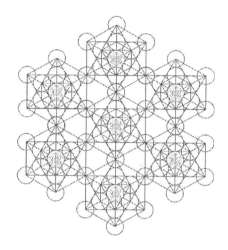

Chapter 10

THE CRASH

Between the ages of 0-7, we program ourselves with the beliefs that best fit our environment at that time.

Remember they are programmed directly into the subconscious mind.

We have over 70,000 thoughts a day most of which have beliefs attached to them. Since there aren't enough pages in this book for the beliefs around 70,000 thoughts, we have simplified the images.

Imagine these beliefs in the six bodies.

These beliefs are creating the movies, and patterns repeating over and over again. Look what happens. The ever-increasing patterns become bigger in density. They distort our vision and point of view.

We get more entangled in this mess over time.

We CAN choose to start detangling at any moment, but we choose not to. We think we are living our lives well.

We BELIEVE we have plenty of time. In reality, we are burying our heads in the sand hoping it will all go away. We think we'll get to that later when we have more time or when we get less busy when the kids are older. Insert whatever excuse fits your circumstance.

We think it is selfish to spend time focusing on ourselves, but, the truth is far from it. It is self-absorbed to stay in our confusion, busyness and distractions. It is this energy and confusion that wears us down: Mentally, Physically, Emotionally and Spiritually.

We have relationships and conversations with other people in similar states of being. We think we are being rational.

We think we are clear on our point of view.

We think we KNOW. We think we are RIGHT. Are we? Aren't we just two people having a conversation running off our automatic programming.

Isn't it THAT programming that we are having a conversation with?

Our conversations, if we are not careful, can end up looking something like this.

As I said, my kids are my most prominent teachers.

A few days after a disagreement with my son, he commented to me, "Mum, do you remember the argument we had the other day? Do you realise in the middle of that argument you said: 'YOU STARTED IT.' How childish!"

I remember laughing at his observation, and happy he hadn't pointed it out in the heat of the moment. He had the presence of mind to wait until a few days later!

"Right," I said when I had finished laughing at myself for coming out with such a ridiculous statement. "I apologise for being so childish. I had better go clear that up!"

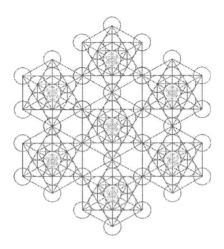

Chapter 11
THE CHOICE

Most of the time we are so entrenched in our programming that we become unaware of what is being said. Have you had a conversation when someone repeats something you have said, and you can't remember saying it?

Most people can relate to arriving at their destination, and can't remember how they got there.

We can continue to bury our heads until we come to a point where we are forced to choose. This is our opportunity to choose LIFE and to LIVE.

This crash comes in the form of a threatening, life-jolting

experience. An accident, severe illness, divorce, bankruptcy, or death of someone who is close to us. You may even have a near-death experience. The specifics can vary, but each CRASH will land you at the very bottom of your despair.

The CRASH forces you to re-evaluate what is important.

I have a friend, Jose Hernandez, who died when he got hit by a bolt of electricity. Fortunately, it was a Near Death Experience. He is now on the Board of IANDS (International Association of Near-Death Studies). NDEs happen a lot more than you think! IANDS has been studying the phenomenon for decades.

I was exploring THE CRASH one day with a dear friend and incredible Life Coach, Shoeleh Forghani. Her dream is to capture people before the crash happens. We discussed why we do not choose to live before we're faced with the possibility of death.

We talked about the material aspect of life and how disconnected people feel from nature. We reach for material things to fill the longing in this void.

Only nature can fill this void.

If only we realised the simplicity in this statement!

We are not comforted in the knowledge that we choose our experiences. Rather we feel trapped in our materialistic lifestyle. Then in this self-entrapment, we go looking for happiness and freedom in external things and people. That can't ever happen. We can only truly experience happiness and freedom from within.

NO EXCEPTION!

Once we HAVE happiness and freedom within, then we get to experience the same in things and people around us!

We think, before the crash, that someone or something else chooses our circumstances FOR us. Therefore, we do not need to take self-responsibility.

If we can blame someone else for our experiences, then we do not have to look internally at what we have created. We don't have to do the necessary work to clean this up. We can keep numbing out and blaming.

If only we could acknowledge that WE CHOOSE everything, that life happens FOR us not TO us.

All we need to do is acknowledge that we create our current circumstances and see that this is our creation. When we do, we can begin to choose new choices that better our circumstances. Then we create more of what we aspire towards and more of what we desire.

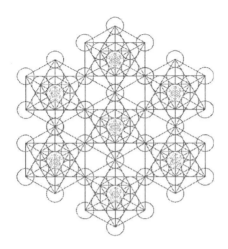

Chapter 12

THE COURAGE IT TAKES

It takes immense courage to be willing to face our beliefs. It can be confronting. We have to be 100% willing to go there. Most of us don't permit ourselves to do this until it's too late to stop the crash.

We must realise that our thoughts from yesterday create our reality today. And our thoughts from today create our reality of tomorrow. Once we understand this, we can start to make the changes necessary in our programming.

We have to look at this programming observationally. We can see with compassion and be fully prepared to forgive. Forgive those around us for helping us create these experiences.

Often the greatest challenge is to forgive our-selves.

The trick to make this easier is to appreciate the exploration of the journey.

If we appreciate, we cannot judge ourselves or anyone else harshly. Appreciation makes it so much easier to assess the programming from an observational point of view. It removes the emotion and judgement.

Then we have to be prepared to wait and be patient with ourselves. Changes in our programming happen instantly, yet it can take time to witness the manifestation of the new programming.

Most of us give up because we are not pre-pared to wait.

We are in an age of instant gratification. We want it NOW! Drive through Fast Food gives us instant dinner. Seemingly a million variations of coffee served in a drive-through loca-tion. You don't even need to leave your car.

Internet shopping now means you don't even need to leave the comfort of your own house or sofa. With a few swipes and clicks, you can order instantly. Get that instant FIX, and it gets delivered to your door for your convenience!

This instant online living has led us to 'miss out' on many opportunities.

For connecting with things and others. The disconnect with others amplifies the disconnect within ourselves. It feeds the need for more instant experiences to soothe the soul. That self-soothing is only temporary though, and also only temporarily feeds the addictions.

The only true way to soothe addictions, and the need to self-soothe with things, is connecting with nature, things, people and animals.

NO EXCEPTION!

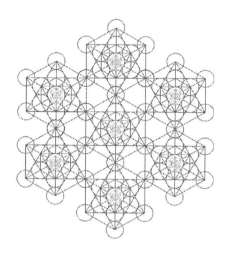

Chapter 13

GOD SHAPED HOLES!

We are trying to fill "God-shaped holes" with Man-shaped objects!

The "God-shaped hole" concept is an innate desire in humans to connect. We try to fill this hole with other things. It's like trying to put a square peg in a round hole. It doesn't quite fit!

The nature of addictions, as I understand it, is through lack of belief and thus connection. Lack of connection with self, things, others and ultimately the Universe. Lack of connection with Universal Power, God, Buddha or whatever else you call the awesome.

When we lose the connection with our cells, our being, we lose connection with our Soul.

Then the cravings begin — for attention and love from others. We can only get attention and love when we have it for ourselves.

I believe that addictions start when we lose belief in others, higher power AND ourselves. When all belief has gone, then we drop into addictions to feed our Soul. Those cravings can never be sustained.

Only the connection to self will feed us, and that starts with belief!

Can you see the cycle?

All we need to do to heal the addictions is to recover the connection to ourselves and those around us. We have to reinstall our belief in ourselves, others, and higher power!

It is difficult for anyone who has HAD a strong belief to understand why people drop into addictions. They ask "Why don't they just STOP?"

Good question!

I believe that we all drop under the **Line of Integrity** from time to time. Those who keep a strong belief can drop down but bounce back up over the line quickly.

I believe that if we lose all belief in self, others and higher power at a young age that's when the trouble begins. We drop all the way down to shame, and we do not have the personal strength and belief in ourselves to elevate. We stay in the lower vibrations. Lose our connections. Later in our life, we have to numb out with addictions to keep ourselves sane! We create our hell.

Have you ever heard an addict's recovery story when they say, "Someone reached out and believed in me?"

Belief is all we need to start lifting ourselves back up the ladder!

The addictions start young when we lose belief in ourselves.

They are subtle and begin with:

· people pleasing
· taking on other's emotions and baggage
· helping
· being on our "best behaviour" so as not to upset people

- biting nails
- escapism
- habits

Habits become habitual and get replaced by addictions as we try to self-soothe.

In this self-soothing process, we create the need to hold on — tight!

We have to hold onto people in case they want to escape from us. We hold onto things, too. We can't let go! We might lose out, and no one likes a loser!

So we hold on tighter and find more things to hold onto. Clasp down tight, and gripping to hold on. By holding on, we begin the process of losing the things we hold dear. Nothing in nature enjoys a strangle-like hold, and every living being and thing does its best to escape you. Holding on hurts your hands, your mind, your body, your muscles and your Soul. It leaves grip marks on your hands — letting go hurts so much less.

One remedy for this is giving. To give the thing that you are craving: love, care, understanding.

"What?!!!" I hear you say, "If I give more won't I have even less of what I have?" It starts with giving to yourself! If you can't manage that, give to others but not until you run dry, only until you can learn to give to yourself.

If you give yourself compassion, then you can fill your own "compassion cup." Fill your cup until it starts to overflow. You can give from the overflow without your cup ever running low or completely depleting!

When you give to others to self-soothe, you have the opposite effect. You deplete your energy and start taking from the person you are trying to help! Have you heard of energy vampires?

If you have enough of something, you can give endlessly, and you will never feel depleted! Simple right?

Give yourself permission. "Prescribe" yourself a good dose of what you are missing. Apply generously until you HAVE enough of it that it overflows to give to others.

In the Bible, Jesus said: "For those who HAVE more will be given, for those who HAVE NOT even what they HAVE will be taken away."

Repeat that out loud and let it soak in.

For those who HAVE more will be given.

When you are in the vibration of HAVING something you attract more of it. The Law of Attraction makes it so! When you have a full cup of anything, you will invite more of it in. You will be able to give more of it, and more will be given!!

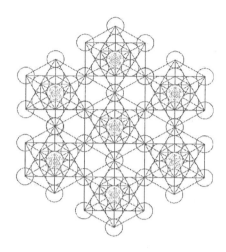

Chapter 14
FREEDOM

Being in the vibration of HAVING brings you more of that thing. The opposite is true. Then you are in the vibration of NOT HAVING — or wanting — what you DO HAVE will be taken away!

This is apparent with money.

Those who have the "air of money" attract more. Those with the air of lack seem to lose their funds as quickly as they receive them!

Lottery winners with a lack mentality will drain all the

money and the relationships around them. Within the next year or so, they've lost everything. It doesn't matter how high the jackpot was.

There is a study to show this truth. Most lottery winners end up being WORSE off after a big win!

It would be better to retain some of the money from a big lottery win to educate the winners with their beliefs around money. With education, they can reinvest and donate that money wisely and be able to give back to society.

Money is a form of energy, and this applies to any energy form.

My youngest son once said to me when he was very young, "Wouldn't it have been better for you not to have me? Then you would have more love for my brother?"

I explained to him that this is not how it works. My love for my second son doesn't get divided with my first son! The love duplicates and amplifies. More is given, and more is received.   Our cup is full and overflowing.

We can give the overflow forever!

It's in the illusion before the crash that keeps us trapped. We stay trapped because we lose the truth. We become engulfed by the promise of more, but if we learn to love what we already have then that love can grow.

When kids "act out" people will say "oh, they need more attention." So you give kids more attention out of guilt and obligation. You become drained and full of hurt feelings, and they act out more!

I believe when kids act out they are asking you to love yourself more and pay more attention to YOURSELF. Then when your cup of attention is full, you can be more present with your kids! Your kids can get the overflow without you running out!

Every action is either Love OR a Request for More Love©.

- Every struggle is a request to love yourself more.
- Every feeling of being trapped is a request to free and love yourself more.
- Every feeling of lack is a request to give to yourself more.

Every low vibration emotion is asking you to pay attention and love yourself more.

Love yourself more. Give more love. Receive more love.

Amplify what we already have. Then we attract more love. We give more and receive more. First, we take the oxygen mask then we can give everyone else the same life-saving breath!

When you have oxygen and space for yourself, you can give breath and HOLD SPACE for others!

All the cells in your body will now be vibrating with this information YES... YES... YES... it's true. Give to us, love us, pay attention to us, and we can take care of you more and more. You can give to the world with the full capacity of your being, and we will never be depleted. We know you will take the necessary steps to care for us, feed us, water us, acknowledge us, forgive us, CONSULT us!

I "ask" my body what it needs, then I give it that thing. I say "Good Morning" to my body of cells every morning, and the cells respond. The trillion of cells "light up" with recognition!

No one likes to be ignored, and neither do our cells. Light them up with a conversation! Out loud or in your head, it doesn't matter. However, no affirmation is more powerful to you than the one said out loud in your own voice. Your voice is coded for your own body to respond to. Say "I AM" out loud and feel that vibration through your chest. Feel the hum!

We get in the way of ourselves with our false programming and view of life. We trip ourselves up in various ways, but that in itself is the brilliance of the way it is. The trips show us what our thoughts and beliefs are. If only we would acknowledge those trips instead of ignoring them, then we could remove the obstacles quickly. We choose to ignore. Yes, this is a choice. We get busy to distract ourselves. We ignore the thing and do more only to trip ourselves up again.

It gets louder and louder and louder until BANG ... the crash happens!

We come to a grinding halt.

"STOP!"

Our inner being shouts louder than we can drown it out.

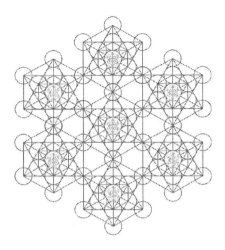

Chapter 15
SURVIVAL

My Crash came in sickness. I awoke one morning saying to myself, "I am not going to survive this."

It was at that point that I actually realised I had a choice. Before that point, believe it or not, I didn't know! I didn't know I had a choice. No one had told me that, and I hadn't discovered it yet for myself.

I was so confronted by that realisation, "What do you mean I have a choice?"

I remember reading personal and spiritual development books. I read about people's stories of transformation and remember willing those experiences to happen to me. It was happening but not in the way I thought it would. I thought I'd have an accident or something dramatic that would make a choice for me. Something that would trans-form me overnight. Something so spectacular that it would force me to think differently! I wanted an EXTERNAL expe-rience to choose for me!

During this realisation, the illusion fell away, and the truth stood glaringly and powerfully before me. It may sound ridiculous, but I honestly didn't know before that point. I thought it would have to be some dramatic climax that would catapult me into existence! I wanted it so badly that I am astonished I didn't manifest it more quickly.

My health scare was, as it turns out, enough!

So I started choosing, reflecting, realising, asking, giving myself more attention. I became more and more aware. I gave myself more choices. Having more choices, allowed me to make more choices and give more choices to those around me.

Every motivational or spiritual speaker has their own story. A story of transformation, some more dramatic than others but they all have a story. Oprah Winfrey, Wayne Dyer, Tony Robbins, Martin Luther King. The greats of all times. Even Jesus had a story of transformation!

Imagine if we do not need a dramatic story for this transformation to happen.

Transformations CAN happen organically.

We can stop and take stock of our lives. We have a choice. We can choose to stay as we are and get sicker and sicker and complain and complain. When we do, we infect those around us. We get more disconnected, lonely, miserable, old and grumpy!

OR we can CHOOSE LIFE — and start living!

My friend and I ask, "Yes, but do we ALL need the crash to see this?"

I think in past times we did need the Crash. We didn't realise we had a choice; we just did what we were programmed to do. The newer generations HAVE more choices, and having the vibration of choice, of course, gives them more options.

We have access to so much more information now, and the

vibration of the collective is getting higher. The collective mind allows us all to HAVE a higher vibration.

It took the discipline and diligence of the new thought leaders. To have the courage and the bravery to go to the depths of the soul that they needed to go to, to make the necessary changes. To demonstrate a better way. So our children can learn this new way and make better choices for themselves.

The minority leaders with enough strength spoke up and said, "This is not the way."

The minority leaders had conviction, self-belief and love.

They had to be brave and strong to speak their truth even when they knew it could harm them.

Those amongst the minority have stood tall and brave. Those who spoke with love pushed through the inertia. This momentum or amplification brings us closer to living in a more harmonious equal environment.

Here we can love ourselves without judgement or conditions, and love others the same way. NO CONDITIONS! NO EXCEPTION!

THE CRASH in itself is a beautiful process and highlights our choice for us.

It is a protection mechanism for survival. We are protecting ourselves from ourselves by crashing.

Most of us have been taught that we don't have a choice. We wouldn't want to be disappointed or let down. Removing the element of choice invites us to conform to the way society wants us to conform. Live by the rules!

My friend once shared a quote from the Baha'i writings that I feel connects well to this concept:

"Regard man as a mine rich in gems of inestimable value. Education can, alone, cause it to reveal its treasures, and enable mankind to benefit there from." — Baha'u'llah

It is astounding that two sentences demonstrate such beauty and wisdom!

We educate ourselves about ourselves to know ourselves intimately when we are brave enough. To mine to our depths for the treasures within, we need to go deep enough to get to the gems of inestimable value. We need to reveal our treasures to benefit humanity, and find our unique gems within. Then we can share them to help humanity.

The Parable of the Talents — Matthew 25:14-30 say a similar thing.

We all have unique gifts and talents to share with the world. We have been gifted them to SHARE, not to keep to ourselves.

Enough of hiding behind the illusion. Enough of keeping our gifts to ourselves for fear of ridicule. Enough of hiding behind insecurities.

It is time RIGHT NOW to mine YOUR precious gems. Dig out your valuable gifts and share them copiously and generously with the world!

How do we do that? Self-awareness.

The next few chapters contain tools and practices to help you "MINE."

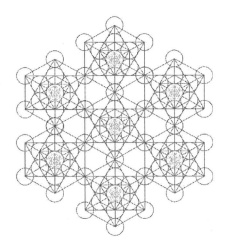

Chapter 16

THE UNENTANGLEMENT

Once you have an awareness of a BELIEF, you can begin the process of "unpacking" it.

The Universe does not like a void and will rush in to fill the void. You need to replace it with something helpful.

Ask yourself permission to do this work.

We create beliefs out of love and protection (even seemingly unhealthy ones)! They worked very well to protect us at some point in our existence.

There may be some resistance to letting go of the old belief. If there is, it is okay!

Remember the gift box I spoke about at the beginning of the book with my ankle injury? Well, this is where you get to use the gift box! If you are unwilling or unable to work on this belief immediately, then intentionally "gift wrap it."

Imagine wrapping this belief up in a beautifully decorated box. Place a bright, colourful ribbon on it, and place it gently on a shelf to review at a later time.

Do remember to go back to it, or it may come crashing down!

Please take care of yourself. If this belief is deeply rooted and you feel unsafe, or uncomfortable, please seek out help to guide you.

It's okay to ask.

Independence comes from within, yet there is also independence in knowing when to ask for help. Be strong enough to have the ability to accept help.

When you do come back to the gift, you will be unwrapping it with curiosity. Look to see what's inside rather than dreading what's to come!

It's so much easier to give yourself space if you are ready to work on something. There is no judgement about this. There is no point rushing things, and everything has a time and place.

My Mum always said, "Go to sleep on a problem, and the solution or answer will be there when you wake up."

If she couldn't work things out immediately then she'd sleep on it. My Mum knew the answers would come through the night.

It's like saying a prayer at the end of the night and review-ing the day and giving blessings. We ask for forgiveness and a solution to a problem. Try it! It works, and there is a scientific explanation. It is called **brain pruning**.

The mind prunes all the solutions that won't work to gives us an answer that will work!

Interestingly when we put our hands together in prayer, we access all the reflexology points in our hands that relate to our whole body.

Once you have permitted yourself and you are willing to

"work" on the belief, you can make a start on the process.

You can intentionally collapse the stack into one to "compress" it. In doing so, it reduces the energy of the impact that this repeating pattern has created.

Intentionally call in the people, animals, nature, objects, environments, experiences and places. Bring in everything that supported you with the core belief.

Acknowledge everyone and everything. Thank them for this experience, for showing up for you in this way, and supporting you with the old belief.

Remember to breathe. You may become a little overwhelmed by what you receive here.

The realisation that these people and things have been showing up FOR you can be a little confronting.

You may have spent a lifetime blaming those people and things for your situation. Remember to be compassionate and kind to yourself through this process.

Once you have acknowledged them, forgiveness is the key to releasing this energy.

IF you are not yet at a place where you are willing to ask them for forgiveness, then stop here. Gift wrap the belief and wait until you can forgive.

My clients often ask, "Why should I ask *them* for forgiveness? Shouldn't it be the other way around?"

This IS the WAY OF SELF-RESPONSIBILITY. The key is to keep moving forward.

Relationships do, however, improve when doing this work. People begin to treat you differently. The outcome here is not to change anyone else or "make" anyone else do anything. It is to improve ourselves and the way we are presenting ourselves to the world.

If you are willing to ask for forgiveness, then please do so! A beautiful and timeless way of doing this is with the **Ho'opo-nopono Prayer**. It is an ancient Hawaiian practice of reconciliation and forgiveness. The word Ho'oponopono translates in English to a correction!

If you haven't heard of the Ho'oponopono, it is worth looking up and reading about Dr Ihaleakala Hew Len. He is a therapist who practised this with an entire ward of criminally insane patients. He 'cured' them without ever meeting any of them, or spending a single moment in the same room! He reviewed each of the patients' notes and healed the judgement in himself!

When we heal ourselves, we allow space for others and the world to heal.

I don't take any credit for healing others. I do not call myself a healer. I facilitate the healing in others through this process of self-awareness.

Don't think that for a moment while you are doing this work that you are selfish or self-centred! This work, although self-focused, is also selfless in affecting the people around you!

The results are astounding.

There may be people in your past who have perceivably wronged or hurt you. I urge you to put them in your awareness and offer yourself this simple prayer. There is nothing wrong in them. They are showing us what wants to be revealed to us.

Please Forgive Me.
I Am Sorry.
Thank You.
I Love You.

It's that simple. Offer it repeatedly until the resistance clears and your thoughts are neutral. Then offer yourself the prayer, too. We all need self-forgiveness!

Holding onto toxic thoughts about someone is like ingesting toxins yourself. You expect the other person to feel it, but the person you hurt most is yourself!

Forgiveness for others and self is a primary key to any self-recovery.

Intentionally "burn" the entanglements between you. I imagine a big vacuum sucking up the fumes and taking it away to be healed. Fill this space with forgiveness, understanding, love, or whatever resonates most with you.

Entanglements are not make-believe!

Neuroscientists and Quantum Physicists have collaborated to prove that the energetic cord between two people exists. There is now a way to record this energy! Like aura imaging, you will soon be able to receive images of the energetic tie between two people!

Remember to forgive yourself for your part in this story. Release all the people, animals, nature, objects, environments, experiences, places.

Set them free and free yourself!

STEP 1

For an example of this process, I lovingly and jokingly use the pretend belief "I am too tall." I can laugh at this very easily, as I am only 5' 1/2"!

To work through this process, I would recite the following:

"I acknowledge each being, thing, place that has supported me in this old belief of I AM TOO TALL. Thank you for showing up for me in this way. I appreciate the part you have played in my story. This story and belief are no longer applicable. I free the cords between us and offer forgiveness prayer. Please Forgive Me. I am Sorry. Thank You. I Love You."

Imagine the entanglement being burnt in your mind's eye. See all the smoke and fumes being sucked into this big vacuum and healed for all time.

"I set you free. I fill the space created with understanding, compassion, acceptance and love."

and then...

"I acknowledge myself for supporting me in this old belief of I AM TOO TALL. Thank you for showing up for me in this way. I appreciate the part I have played in my own story.

This story and belief are no longer applicable. I free myself from this entanglement. I offer the forgiveness prayer of: Please Forgive Me. I am Sorry. Thank You. I Love You."

You should feel much lighter after releasing all that energetic weight!

Continue to <u>Step 2</u> of this process.

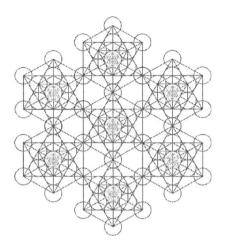

Chapter 17

EXERCISES FOR THE MENTAL BODY

STEP 2

In my private practice with clients, I use a system called *Sequence of Senses©*. It is the sequence we prefer to remember information with our senses.

I assess the client for the sequence in which they prefer to use their senses. For this practice, we will use a generic sequence. It works just as well; however, your mind may take a second longer to "translate" the information! Take your time and be patient.

Close your eyes and take a couple of deep breaths. Make yourself comfortable in a quiet place. Take your attention to your mind and send a request to view all the experiences about your old belief.

You may recall a flash of experiences. Take care not to judge each one, but notice them with as much neutrality as possible. If this gets uncomfortable, stop and reach out for someone to help you.

Once the experiences have slowed, you can ask your mind to "show you the belief." You will see the words of the belief you are working on, for example, "I AM TOO TALL."

See words in your mind. If they are moving, press pause and have them come to a still point.

Then shrink the words. Make them smaller and smaller in your mind's eye. Drain all colours associated with these words. Make them smaller and smaller until they are hardly discernible.

Notice the voice inside your head reciting your words. Mentally turn down the volume in your head. Imagine a volume switch. Turn it down until you can no longer hear it.

I had one client say to me, "Can I do that?" To which I

answered, "Of course you can. It's your choice, remember?"

Drain any tastes or smells associated with these words. Imagine them being sucked up into the vacuum to be healed. Any feelings that come up at this point can also be sucked into this vacuum.

Replace your words with new ones to create a new belief. The replacement is usually the opposite of the belief you are replacing. Ask yourself, and it will come to you! For example, you may choose something like, "*I AM perfect just the way I am.*"

Recite the new belief out loud. Remember your voice and your vibration is a powerful command tool.

Make the new words bigger and bigger. Bring them in closer. Add colour, lots of it! Turn up the volume on the volume control. Make it louder and louder. Recite it out loud three times so you can hear yourself say it!

Bring in tastes, smells and breathe this new belief into your mind. Take three deep breaths and intentionally "*breathe them into your brain.*" You will feel your brain calming.

Write the new belief down to reinforce it!

I use sticky notes to write the new belief on. I put one on my bathroom mirror, on my desk, above my bed, and even in my car.

Recite the new belief to yourself at night before you go to sleep.

Do it again first thing in the morning!

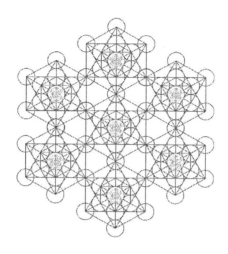

Chapter 18

EXERCISES FOR THE PHYSICAL BODY

STEP 3

Begin in a quiet place and make yourself comfortable.

Think about the old belief as you scan your body. Where do you feel it? Ask your body to tell you where you notice this belief.

You may feel some resistance somewhere in your body. You may feel, tight, sore, painful, hot, itchy or agitated. Don't judge the reaction. Just notice it.

Then drop into this resistance further, deeper into the centre of where you feel it. Allow yourself to sit with it. If it gets too uncomfortable, ask it to release the tension.

Notice how it feels. Notice the feeling, the colour, and sensation.

Ask, *"What is the message around this belief?"*

What information do you receive? You may be surprised by the answer.

Feel the energy around the belief in your body. Imagine a speck of light right in the centre of this energy and breathe into it. Feel it vibrate. Feel it getting warmer or cooler. Keep breathing into it and watch the colour and texture dilute.

Breathe into this light until it expands enough to replace the old sensation, colour and texture. Then breathe this light into your whole body repeating the new belief, *"I am perfect just the way I am."*

Feel the light expand into your whole body each time you recite your new belief.

If you feel excessive pain or discomfort, "gift wrap" the belief and shelve it until a later date.

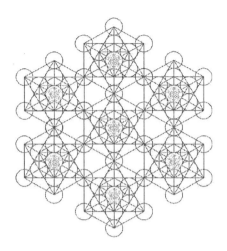

Chapter 19

EXERCISES FOR THE EMOTIONAL BODY

STEP 4

Be prepared to get emotional with this exercise.

Think about the old belief and let yourself feel how it felt to have this old belief. Notice the first emotion to come to the surface and acknowledge it!

"Thank you (NAME THE EMOTION) for being my internal compass. I am sorry for ignoring this feeling. It is safe to feel this emotion now."

Let yourself feel this emotion until it eases.

Then ask the question, "*What layer of emotion is underneath this (NAME THE FIRST EMOTION)?*"

Then allow yourself to feel this second layer of emotion.

If you feel the urge to cry, it's okay. Let yourself cry. Did you know that when we cry, our tears contain hormones? We are detoxing our system when we shed tears!

Repeat this process with each layer of emotion. Keep repeating until you run out of layers. You will notice at the last layer you just run out. Either that or you start feeling a more helpful emotion.

Allow yourself a minute to breathe and reflect on those feelings. Intentionally see them being sucked into the vacuum to be healed.

After a minute, let yourself feel what the new belief feels like and say, "*I am perfect just the way I am.*" Recite three times with three breaths while feeling the amazing feeling of the new belief spreading throughout your body.

Remember to be compassionate and kind to yourself. Ask for support if you need it.

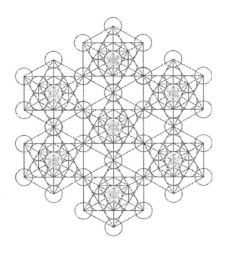

Chapter 20

EXERCISES FOR THE SPIRITUAL BODY

STEP 5

Visit the stories around the old belief. Acknowledge how this belief served you well at some point!

You can write the story out, or replay it in your mind. Know you are just "visiting" it from an observational perspective.

You can see this story from the new perspective of your new belief. Then you can see the truth in the old belief.

"I can see now how having that belief of being too tall sup-ported me. Now I can lovingly let all the stories around this belief be stored and filed as they are no longer need-ed."

Imagine a book with the title of the old belief. Fill this book with all the experiences that flashed before you around this belief. Intentionally "fill" this book with all of these experi-ences. See them with wonder.

How brilliant we are for creating these expe-riences!

Slip these experiences into the book, and complete each page one at a time. Once the experiences have filled the blank pages of this book, you can flip to the back of the book and notice the last page. Does is feel completed? Can you see the words "The END," or something to that effect? If so, intentionally ask that it be completed and filed in the appropriate place.

Rewrite the story, but from your new perspective with the new belief. Notice the subtle but powerful changes in your story.

Write a paragraph about how you would respond different-ly if one of these stories repeated in any way.

1. *What would you see?*

2. *How would you see it?*

3. *What would you do?*

4. *What would you say?*

If you have a verbal response, say it out loud. Act out a scene so you know with 100% certainty that you have an appropriate response that makes you feel completely comfortable and confident! When it happens the next time, the new response is automatic and then the patten falls away.

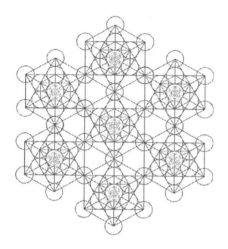

Chapter 21

EXERCISES FOR THE INTERNAL BODY

STEP 6

Changing your perception internally is an essential part of this process.

How you feel about yourself internally is PRESENTED to the outside world.

We think that if we keep our internal perception of ourselves to ourselves, then it is private. However, it's not. It is written all over your face. It's shown in your expressions. People hear it in your tone of voice. You demonstrate your internal world through the posture of your body and gestures!

So remember, when you're thinking lower vibrational thoughts about yourself, you are externalising them also.

Remember the old belief, and see how you saw yourself with that old belief internally! How do you see that internal representation? With its old feelings now drained, how does this image look to you? Dated? Old? Worn? Tired? Tattered?

Now see this image of how you see yourself internally, and scrunch that image up into a tiny ball. Shrink it further until it's a tiny dot. Then imagine it being sucked into the vacuum to be carried away to be healed.

Then bring out a new internal image. Create a new picture in your mind about how you see yourself with the new images of the new belief. Use all your senses to heighten this image's colour, size, shape, sounds, feelings, tastes, and smells.

Take some time for yourself to journal the new image you have of yourself. What are the new things you are saying to yourself?

I am perfect just the way I am!

How does it feel to have this new image?

Take your time to do this. Really feel what it feels like from an internal perspective to have this new image of yourself.

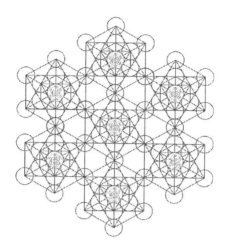

Chapter 22

EXERCISES FOR THE EXTERNAL BODY

<u>STEP 7</u>

Close your eyes and intentionally see a full-length mirror in front of you. See the reflection of yourself and what you look like from an external perspective.

What do other people see?

What do you notice with the image of yourself with the old belief?

Imagine that reflection is old and covered in dust. Now see yourself reach out to this mirror and wipe the mirror clean. As you are rubbing the mirror clean, you see a new reflection! A new reflection with the new belief you have chosen.

This image sees a brighter you with brighter colours. You are standing a little taller and looking a little younger. Refreshed! Notice your complexion. It seems healthier. Overall you just look better!

Hear what others are saying to you.

Who are your cheerleaders? What are they saying?

Are there any smells or tastes associated with this new image? If so, breathe them in. Remember them. Feel the new belief inside you taking form! Take a mental "picture" of that person, and keep it front of mind.

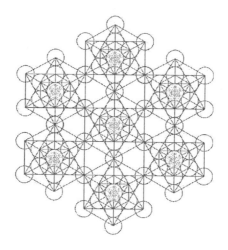

Chapter 23

RELATIONSHIPS

This process is a detox.

Take care of yourself. Rest. Journal. Drink lots of fresh filtered water. An Epsom salts bath is always a good idea. ASK for support from those around you and your guides.

You receive help when you ask for it.

Sometimes I am shown things in my dreams, simple ways to see things differently, to simplify the complicated. I was given the Rubix Cube analogy one night to explain the complexity of our different viewpoints.

When we look at a situation from one viewpoint, we only see one colour! You may see red while I see blue! We are both right about the colour we see.

People's observations of life are like a Rubix Cube!

If we angle the cube (or the experience) just a little, we may see two colours. Again, we may both see two different colours, neither right nor wrong. If we take the cube and turn it around to look at it from all perspectives, we may be surprised to see there are six colours! When we see the whole cube or the whole perspective, we see the entire story!

It's the same with relationships. We see it one way while the other person sees it another. Neither is right or wrong. It's just the way it IS.

There is no need to change the viewpoint if it is healthy for everyone involved. I explain to my kids that something is only fun if it is fun for everyone.

What if we do not like the viewpoint?

Now, there's a different story! We rant and we rave about how people are treating us, and how we don't deserve to be treated that way.

How dare they?

Then we repeat the story to someone else. We choose someone who we know will agree with us. (We don't want to be wrong!) That person will delve into the story with us. We both decide and reinforce our belief about that behaviour being wrong!

"See!" We say, "I am RIGHT!"

What if the Rubix cube is angled slightly? Do we get a different viewpoint? Probably!

If we are willing to pick up that Rubix Cube and look at it from all angles, we may realise the story is happening FOR us.

Every time someone demonstrates a particular behaviour that stings, it's showing up FOR us every time!

NO EXCEPTION!

They may be stepping over our boundaries, and that may upset us. That only happens when we don't know what our values and limitations are! We teach others how to treat us by the way we treat ourselves.

The behaviour that stings is shown to us in one of three ways!

1. It is showing us what we don't want and that we haven't yet got clear about what we do want.
2. The behaviour is a reflection of what is inside of US, but we don't want to see!
3. The behaviour is triggering something inside of us that is a memory of something that happened in the past. It is something we are projecting onto the here and now!

How do we figure out what we want in relationships, and what our boundaries are? We will dig a little deeper into these examples in the next three exercises.

EXERCISES
1. DON'T WANT vs DO WANT

When you ask yourself what you want in a relationship, you are not clear. You are clear, however, about what you DON'T want. You may have lots of experience with that!

The Law of Attraction brings you more of the same — stuff you don't want! Knowing what you don't want helps you get clear about what you do want!

This first exercise is a way to focus on the type of healthy relationships that you do want.

Draw six columns on a piece of paper.

Column #1

List what you don't want. It is easy to recall what you don't want. Keep listing until you run out!

Column #2

List what you DO want. Usually the opposite of what you don't want!

Did your Mum say to you as a child, "I want, I want... never gets!"? Well, she was right! "I WANT" keeps you in the energy of wanting and never get-ting! So we have to expand to another statement.

Column #3

List examples of where you have seen this thing you want in others. Then you have the evidence that it IS possible.

Column #4

List the examples of where you have seen this happen for yourself. If you have no examples, then list a possibility for it to happen.

Column #5

Create an I AM, I HAVE, and I BELIEVE statement to be in the vibration of the here and now and in a vibration of HAVING.

Column #6

ASK for help! Whether you are asking your guides, the Universe or people for support, it doesn't matter. Just ASK.

DON'T WANT	DO WANT	HAS ANYONE ACHIEVED THIS?	CAN YOU SEE A TIME YOU HAVE HAD IT?	CREATE I AM, I HAVE, I BELIEVE STATEMENTS
Poor Relationship	*Healthy Relationships*	*Yes, my friend*	*Yes, I have had healthy relationships before.*	*I am in a healthy relationship. I have a healthy relationship. I believe I can create a healthy relationship.*

EXERCISES

2. REFLECTIONS

The next exercise is a little more challenging, so be gentle with yourself.

A couple of years ago I reflected on a troubled relationship. This person had bullied me so much over the years. I suddenly realised with a thump that that person had actually been showing up for me in a beautifully, perfect way! They had been showing up for me by bullying me just a little bit more than I was bullying myself!!!

AND THAT WAS A LOT!

WOW! I couldn't believe the realisation as it hit me. I was on a beach and cried right there on the spot. I cried and cried tears of sorrow for how badly I had treated myself. How badly others had treated me. How badly I had misunderstood the situation. I felt so sorry for myself!

Then I realised there was not a thing to be sorry for, and I could feel wonderful about all of this!

This behaviour was triggering me to pay attention and show me my beliefs. If I didn't like it, I could change it at any time!

I asked for help from my guides.

How can I transform this relationship for us both? It wasn't an intimate relationship, and I didn't see this person very often, but the behaviour still affected me!

I got my answer: **FORGIVENESS**!

I received this written exercise to help me transform this relationship.

Thank you for showing up for me by BULLYING me just a little bit more than I am BULLYING myself.

Thank you for showing up for me in a way that I couldn't see for myself.

You no longer need to show up for me in this way, as I will no longer treat myself this way.

Please forgive me. I am sorry. Thank you. I love you.

I forgive myself for bullying myself this way, and for the false perception that this was happening TO me.

The behaviour had highlighted the belief that "I deserved to be bullied!"

How beautiful life can be!

I didn't need to say anything out loud to that person to heal this, but I did.

The next time I spoke to them I merely said, "Thank you for showing up for me!" No explanation. No excuses. No justifications. Just a simple, heartfelt thank you!

That person has shown up for me with kindness ever since!

I went a little mad for the next few weeks. I bought a journal and wrote this out to everyone I could remember whose behaviour had ever stung me! There was a lot.

- That person who was two-faced.
- That person who abandoned me.
- That person who was mean to me.
- That person who was bitchy!!!

ALL OF THEM SHOWING UP FOR ME! THANK YOU!

Once I had dried up the pen and filled the pages of be-haviours that had stung me, another realisation hit me. I could see the things I admired in people! They were also showing up for me in ways that I couldn't show up for my-self.

- The person who was so beautiful showed me the beauty in myself!
- The person who loved so profoundly showed me I had that same capacity!
- The person who was so courageous showed me I was also courageous!

Thank you to everyone who demonstrated all of the per-ceivably good or bad behaviours to me.

EXERCISES
3. PAST EXPERIENCES, CURRENT REALITY

Past experiences create our current reality.

There is part of your brain that stores past experiences, and dictates how you respond to the present situation.

If the previous experience was peaceful, it would have you respond peacefully. The PreFrontal Cortex is activated and produces oxytocin and other calming chemicals.

If the previous experience was not peaceful, the Amygdala, or the Primate Brain, is activated and produces Cortisol and other not so peaceful chemicals.

We have to learn how to HAVE and hold space for ourselves before we can have and hold space for others.

Knowing we have six responses to feeling unsafe helps you to understand your reactions.

My practice called *Sequence of Safety©* is where we find out which of the following responses comes in which order.

The six responses are as follows:

1. **FIGHT**: Ready to attack or be defensive.
2. **FLIGHT**: Where we take off to another physical area, or in our mind. ("Away with the fairies," one might say!)
3. **PLEASE/APPEASE**: Where we will try to appease ourselves or the other person, by saying, "Oh it's ok, don't worry about it." See how people pleasing can hurt us? It has the same chemical reaction in us as being in fight mode!
4. **FREEZE**: Where we literally freeze in one spot.
5. **VICTIM**: Why is this happening to me? The Why becomes WHIIIINNNNEEEE as my NLP Instructor, Steve Boyley, would say in a whiny voice. It certainly got the point across!
6. **VICTIMIZING**: Where we exclaim, "Screw you!" Or we'd threaten or punish the other person.

These six responses happen in everyone!

NO EXCEPTION!

We all have them in varying degrees of severity and different orders.

Observe yourself to understand the order of your own six responses. You may then calibrate and catch yourself before you escalate to ALL SIX.

I will give you an example of how this works with me. My order is Freeze, Flight (out of my mind), Please/Appease, Fight, Victim, Victimize.

Here's an example of an uncomfortable situation for me. My kids are starting an argument in front of me. My six responses would go something like this:

1. **FREEZE**: I freeze on the spot. I try to assess my situation and find ways to make this safe. I can feel my brain freeze while trying to search for a way out of danger.
2. **FLIGHT**: Arguing is a trigger for me. I don't like to see people fighting especially my kids. My brain stored the information at an early age that people arguing is NOT SAFE. My brain is firmly sticking to that story! My mind goes into the dream state of *'away with the fairies.'*
3. **APPEASE/PLEASE**: Pllleeeeaaassse stop! You don't need to argue! We can find another way.
4. **FIGHT**: "JUST STOP IT NOW!"
5. **VICTIM**: "Really, why are you doing this?" Remember the whhhyyyynnnnninnng!
6. **VICTIMIZE**: "RIGHT! If you don't stop this RIGHT now I am going to blah, blah, blah."

'WHY' is a very good question, if we use it as a starting

point, but don't stay there. Shifting gears from "Why is this happening to me?" to "How can this serve me?" or "What is it teaching me?" is a really good practice.

My kids know what my responses are. They know when I am threatening the removal of electronics that I am on my very last reaction of not feeling safe!

They get it so they can stay out of their own responses!

When we have escalated through our responses all we are saying is blah, blah, blah — and all the other person is hearing is blah, blah, blah, blah.

There really isn't any point in furthering conversation at this stage. We would be better to stop talking and wait until we have all calmed down.

A good way of NOT going back into the heated argument is to ask permission first. "Is now a good time to talk about this, or would you like to talk about it later?"

If the answer is "NO, it's not a good time" learn to accept this gracefully and leave it for another time. If now is a good time, try to stay out of your reactions so you can hold space.

Actively listen to what's being said.

I got excited when I understood these six responses and started observing the people around me. A car screeched out in front of me on a two-lane highway. I put my foot on the brake and stopped the vehicle. I FROZE. The guy next to me started beeping his horn and using THE finger. He was in FIGHT and VICTIMIZE.

I started paying more attention to my reactions.

A few years ago I had to watch a 30-minute training video. I didn't want to watch it, and I was forcing myself to do something I didn't want to do. When it got to the end, I realised I hadn't "seen" a single second of it! I started again. Halfway through I realised the same thing. I stopped the video and had a conversation with myself.

I gave the Amygdala a character. His name is Dexter the Dinosaur. Dexter is from a kids book that I used to read to my kids when they were little. It is called *Dexter and Daisy's Day Out* by Nick Sharratt.

I had a conversation with Dexter. It went something like this, "Hey Dexter, I can see you have come out of your cave, and you are starting to activate the defence operation. What are you feeling scared about?"

The answer was clear, "Home is not safe."

I was shocked at Dexter's answer.

"Really, you think it's not safe at home? Where did you ever get that idea from?"

Somewhere, somehow between the ages of 0-7, I had decided that home wasn't safe and adopted it as a belief.

It may have been when there was a family argument or when the neighbours used to fight, and we could hear it through our thin walls. Or the belief may have come from someone else entirely.

It doesn't matter where it originated. What does matter is that it was still affecting me as an adult! I flashed through all the experiences where I had perceived that I wasn't safe at home. I had always wondered why I was much more effective in a workplace than I was at home.

Dexter had literally been on "High Alert" every time I was at home, and I was utterly oblivious to it!

Giving Dexter a name and a character helped me have that conversation. Immediately when I think of Dexter, I get warm and fuzzy, peaceful memories of reading to my kids. It switches gear straight away leaving me able to "dig the mine for the jewels."

I said, "Thank you, Dexter. Thank you for keeping me safe and on high alert, but you can relax now. Home IS safe so you can go back into your cave and pull the covers up in your bed and go back to sleep."

I would see this happen in my mind.

I had to "reset" my brain with another belief that home is safe.

I would have a conversation with the part of my brain that stores past experiences. I gave that a character, too.

My character is Gloria the Hippopotamus from the movie Madagascar. "Hey Gloria, how are you today? I see you got the message that home wasn't safe. Well, you know what? There has been a software upgrade. Please upgrade that programming now and run the software update with "Home IS Safe!" Inform Dexter of the update and let all the other parts of the brain know that it is safe to play at home!"

"Sure" Gloria would say in my imagination and wiggle her hips off to do her new duty.

It may sound crazy talking to yourself like that, but it works!

Why not create your own characters around the parts of your brain?

I believe Neuroscientists have been focusing on studying the prefrontal cortex more in the past decade because collectively we have just started developing and using this part of our brain more.

Most of us have been living with Dexter driving from the Prehistoric Brain, the Amygdala, without a driver's license or instructions on how to drive.

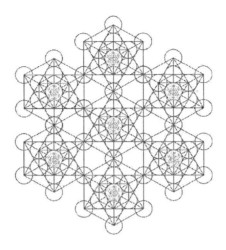

Chapter 24

SELF-AWARENESS

I appreciate the level of awareness writing this book has taught me! It has instilled a new sense of freedom, one I'd like to share with the world.

Consider the possibility that we return to a childlike state! Not the CHILDISH way we behave. Nor the children we were past the age of seven when we already had 90% of our programming.

The TRUE childlike self.

Imagine seeing everything through the eyes of a child with simplicity.

A child knows only unconditional love, kindness and compassion. To receive that we have to BE that for ourselves!

- Be a child who gets to play.
- Be utterly unconcerned about what others think.
- Be in a state of joy that delights our cells and allows us to love even more.
- Be like a baby learning to walk. We get up when we fall. We wipe our tears. We laugh and take another step forward!

Remember we do not learn to walk with just one step. Be consistent and patient with yourself as you transition through the layers of beliefs.

A previous mentor of mine, Maitraya Joy, would say to me it is like an onion skin. Be patient with each belief and peel the onion one layer at a time.

Be generous, like a child.

Make sure your family and friends know you BELIEVE in them. Be that ONE person who holds BELIEF for others and the change in the world! Saying "I believe in you" is one of the most precious gifts you can give to anyone.

- I believe you have all the resources you require.
- I believe you always have the best intentions at heart!
- I believe everyone is doing the best they can at that moment in time.

I have a desire to make a significant impact in the world with simple solutions that allow us all to connect to our true childlike self — where we get to play no matter what we do!

If anything, be childlike.

To all the children out there — young and old — I love you!

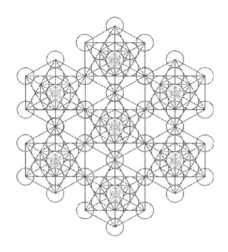

Chapter 25

A LITTLE OF MY OWN STORY

I am an ordinary girl from Barnsley, that was an ordinary coal mining town in Yorkshire, England. I am ordinary but special.

I have an ordinary family and friends all over the world. They are ordinary and special, too.

If I can make it through this journey, anyone can.

You just have to believe it is so, and take action to do the processes to make it happen.

We are all ordinary and special at the same time. We each have our unique signature and stamp for the world.

My journey wasn't always easy. I am an experiential learner and had to learn the hard way by experiencing it.

I know the journey in this book because I have experienced it! I lost belief in myself, others and a higher power as a young child.

I replaced my unhealthy cravings with healthy ones. One at a time until the healthy addictions fell away and were no longer needed. It is far easier to replace an addiction than try to stop it.

I had stumbled into addictions starting with people pleasing as a child. I dropped down to addictions hidden in shame. With the material in this book, I left them behind one at a time. My last layer of addiction was people pleasing. It makes sense that the first layer was the final layer I had to release! It was probably the hardest to let go of. I had to climb my way back up the emotional scale above the line of integrity once again.

My journey began with a choice to be a better person today than I was yesterday. I seek to be an even better person tomorrow than I am today.

Educating myself about myself was just as important as the formal education I had received.

Your journey may hold similar experiences as mine did in the self-help movement. You may have attended weekend retreats, joined meditation circles, practised yoga, and had sessions with different practitioners. You may have followed spiritual leaders or listened to channellers or intuitive readers. It all helps you along your way.

I even experienced firewalking and loved it! I thought I would never have the courage to step on burning hot coals, but I did ... three times!

My daily rituals and affirmations are things I aspire to.

I have experienced all of this, but my most significant discoveries have been on my own.

For example, remember my trail running on a remote mountain with my dog? It may have been extreme, but it was how I needed to experience me.

You have to find your unique way to experience yourself.

At one point during my running, I realised I was my own

best friend and that I finally DID love and respect myself! I realised I COULD connect to myself and my higher self.

ANYONE can meditate at the top of a mountain. I had to learn to be in a similar state no matter what my circumstances were or who I was with. Then I had to apply it to everyday life!

At first, I had to "bubble" myself with an imaginary bubble of light. A bubble with a wall so thick a laser wouldn't get through!

I can now be a responsible empath and go to places packed with people and remain calm. I let the energies pass through me.

When I reflect on my journey, I realise how blessed I've been. I've travelled the world and lived in three different countries. I had a relationship with a man for 23 years, and although our marriage ended, I am lucky enough to call him one of my best friends. I have two awesome children that mean the world to me.

I had to scrap most of the beliefs I had about myself. They were beliefs that prevented me from appreciating things and people. They stopped me from enjoying the world. I had to rebuild those beliefs with healthy ones that allowed me to appreciate life.

I had to discover myself to HAVE strong and healthy beliefs in myself.

The belief starts in others. I sought out people who I admired and who helped me. I read books and watched Youtube videos. I followed others who I believed in, although sometimes to my detriment. At least I believed in someone!

Until one day I began to believe in myself. I held my belief in others, but I didn't need to follow anyone anymore.

The coincidences were just too many, conversations too profound, and the alignments too synchronistic to NOT to believe in a higher power.

I asked to have a closer connection with myself and with a Universal Higher Power. I received what I asked for, and the connection became deeper every day.

I only need to step out into nature to notice the communications around me.   On January 1st I hiked alone on a remote pathway and asked for confirmation and guidance.

I turned a corner and saw the most magnificent sight. There was an eagle on a tree right in front of me. He was so close and stayed perfectly still. As he looked me in the eye, I was overwhelmed with gratitude. The message I'd been seeking was confirmed.

When I got home, I looked up the significance of an eagle and found this:

"Eagle conveys the powers and messages of the spirit; it is man's connection to the divine because it flies higher than any other bird. If an eagle has appeared, it bestows freedom and courage to look ahead. The eagle is symbolic of the importance of honesty and truthful principles."

It gave me the courage to look ahead!

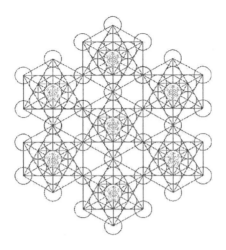

Chapter 26
SUPPORT SYSTEMS

The lessons are all around us.

There are signs and information in every conversation. IF we take the time and awareness to realise this is true.

My family and friends, and every interaction, showed me.

I encourage you to choose friends who hold you account-able for your truth. Ones who will embrace you when you need it. There is nothing more valuable than a friend who can hold space for you without judgement.

- A friend who elevates you to the higher emotions, and encourage self-responsibility.
- A friend who won't follow you into your drama story who agrees with you and amplifies it to make it worse.
- A true friend stays out of their drama when you drop into yours.
- A true friend tells you when you are sabotaging yourself by staying in the weakness of the emotions under the line of integrity.
- A true friend has the grace to love you and be truthful, no matter what.

Every person who you encounter has the potential to be a true friend.

I would call my friends from time to time and ask, "Can you please give me some time and space to complain?"

They would listen politely, but not take any heed of what I was actually saying. They would let me complain just long enough to find my way back out of the fog. Back to a brighter place where I could reclaim self-responsibility.

When you are struggling to be your own best friend find someone who can lift you up for you to heal.

I do not call myself a HEALER. The work I do facilitates healing in others. You are the HEALER for healing. We can heal ourselves. Find a way of believing in your powers of self-healing.

I am my own spiritual leader. Be your own spiritual leader.

Find your spiritual path.

I have found a way to believe and connect. Find your way.

I have found a higher power to believe in. Find yours.

With love and blessings,
Marie

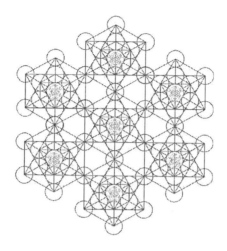

EPILOGUE

FROM THE MOUTHS OF BABES

My son was only five when he told me how his dreams taught him about the energetic nature of all.

He mentioned Metatron as one of the teachers!

Amongst other things, he taught me how trees communicate with each other — and with us. This knowledge was profound, and the conversation was well beyond the years of this five-year-old child. He had my attention.

Around the same time, I started seeing orbs in photos.

I watched my son play on a beach one day, quietly and gracefully.

He was moving in Tai Chi-like movements, even though he had never studied Tai Chi. I took photos of him and was captivated by his movements. I was startled to see the orb he was seemingly commanding.

Is it possible he was communicating with a being who we couldn't see?

Let's stop missing precious moments and be childlike with the children around us.

Children are our teachers and our future.

Let us see what they teach us.   Let us be open to discover what a wonderful world they can create.

ABOUT THE AUTHOR

Marie Martin guides clients to find their child-like spark. It is the child-like self before the programming tarnished their perception of the world.

Marie is a problem solver who helps you discover your true purpose and possibilities with simple solutions that make a big impact on the world.

The creator of the best-selling book, *Metatron's Code*, Marie discovered the techniques that she used to heal herself. She continues to use these processes daily in her own life and with clients. This book demystifies our belief systems, and guides you to deactivate harmful beliefs to re-create a belief. The next expansion of the Metatron's Code has already begun and will be available along with a children's book.

Marie Martin speaks on belief systems and the six bodies that are required to re-code to create simplicity and space in life.

Amongst Marie's qualifications are the following:

Bachelor's Degree in Metaphysical Science,
Master NLP (Neuro Linguistic Programming) Practitioner &
Certified Communications Specialist
Certified Regression Healing Hypnosis with the Quantum
Healing Centre
Conversational Intelligence® for Coaches Enhanced Skill
Practitioner
HeartMath Facilitator
Ho'oponopono Practitioner

She continues her studies in Universal Law Coaching Certi-
fication with Joy Kingsborough.

To connect with Marie:

www.mariemartincoaching.com
www.metatronscode.com